RSPB
Pocket Book of
Hedgehogs

RSPB
Pocket Book of
Hedgehogs

Hugh Warwick

BLOOMSBURY WILDLIFE
LONDON · OXFORD · NEW YORK · NEW DELHI · SYDNEY

The RSPB Pocket Book series invites readers to explore the deeper and wilder worlds of some of our most familiar and beloved wild species. We take a deep but undaunting dive into their lives and ways, their evolution and anatomy, and their resonance and value to us in our own lives, from our earliest depictions of their form to the ways that we are working to safeguard them and their habitats for the future.

The *RSPB Pocket Book of Hedgehogs* celebrates these most charming, enigmatic and beloved inhabitants of our gardens, hedgerows and woodlands. We begin by looking at the evolutionary history of hedgehogs, then explore their private lives, from what and how they eat to their breeding behaviour, hibernation, travels and lifespan. We take a look at hedgehogs' importance in human cultures across their global range and through written history, and finally we learn what we can do to help hedgehogs in the British Isles to recover from their recent population decline and thrive across our gardens and countryside once again.

Hugh Warwick is an ecologist and author who specialises in hedgehogs. His books include *A Prickly Affair*, *Cull of the Wild*, *Linescapes*, and guides to hedgehogs and beavers.

BLOOMSBURY WILDLIFE
Bloomsbury Publishing Plc
50 Bedford Square, London, WC1B 3DP, UK
Bloomsbury Publishing Ireland Limited,
29 Earlsfort Terrace, Dublin 2, Ireland

BLOOMSBURY, BLOOMSBURY WILDLIFE and the Diana logo
are trademarks of Bloomsbury Publishing Plc

First published in the United Kingdom 2026

A catalogue record for this book is available from the British Library
Library of Congress Cataloguing-in-Publication data has been applied for

ISBN: HB: 978-1-3994-2921-4; ePub: 978-1-3994-2924-5

2 4 6 8 10 9 7 5 3 1

Design by Austin Taylor
Printed and bound in Great Britain by Clays Ltd, Elcograf S.p.A.

MIX
Paper | Supporting
responsible forestry
FSC® C018072
www.fsc.org

To find out more about our authors and books, visit www.bloomsbury.com
and sign up for our newsletters
For product-safety-related questions, contact productsafety@bloomsbury.com

Published under licence from RSPB Sales Limited to raise awareness of the RSPB
(charity registration in England and Wales no 207076 and Scotland no SC037654)

For all licensed products sold by Bloomsbury Publishing Limited, Bloomsbury
Publishing Limited will donate a minimum of 2% from all sales to RSPB Sales Ltd,
which gives all its distributable profits through Gift Aid to the RSPB

Contents

CHAPTER ONE

Introducing Hedgehogs

If there is one animal in the British Isles that you could count on most people identifying, it would be the hedgehog. Famously prickly, in appearance if not character, the hedgehog has forgone the insulating fur of most other mammals, and evolved defensive prickles. If you have ever met a hedgehog and paid close attention, you will know how sharp those prickles can be, even though they are just modified hair.

What is a hedgehog?

. . . .

Hedgehogs belong to the mammal order called Eulipotyphla. This grouping also includes shrews and moles – furry mammals, but like hedgehogs they are sharp-toothed eaters of insects and other invertebrates. The porcupines are another famous group of spiny mammals, but they are rodents, related to mice and squirrels. If we look at the wider animal world, there are the sea urchins – also famously spiny, and although they are invertebrates, they have more in common with hedgehogs than you might think. The name 'urchin' is the old name for hedgehog, so by name these sea creatures are 'sea hedgehogs'.

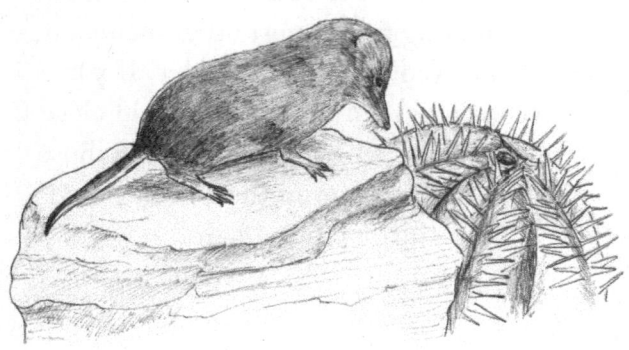

The echidnas of Australasia have hedgehog-like prickles and are sometimes known as 'spiny anteaters'. However, these strange egg-laying mammals are not related to hedgehogs at all, or indeed to the 'true' anteaters, despite the best-known species (the Short-beaked Echidna, found across Australia) feeding mainly on ants. Spines are an effective way of keeping protected from predators, and as such have evolved in various unrelated animal groups – this is known as 'convergent evolution'. There are a few other mammals that are, in evolutionary terms, perhaps also considering arming up. The spiny mice and spiny rats have evolved stiff, pointed hairs and may, if left to their own devices and given a few million years, become fully prickly!

The Western European Hedgehog

. . . .

There are up to 19 species of spiny hedgehogs around the world – taxonomists are continually changing their minds – though only one of these lives in the wild in the British Isles. This book will focus just on this species, *Erinaceus europaeus*, the Western European Hedgehog. We may consider it 'our' hedgehog, but it is actually found all the way from the west coast of Ireland to the Czech

Republic and from Norway to Spain. The other hedgehog species are found across Eurasia to the east coast of China, and south through Africa to South Africa. The hedgehogs in New Zealand are Western European Hedgehogs and are there because nineteenth-century colonists from Europe were not aware of the consequences of introducing new and exotic species to this far-flung country. There are no wild hedgehogs in the Americas, but some African species are kept there as pets.

The British have a rather special relationship with *Erinaceus europaeus*. Every time there is a vote or a poll for the nation's favourite wild mammal, or nature icon, the hedgehog wins. (This upsets many of my ornithological friends.)

The prickles on the hedgehog are one of the key reasons why we have formed such a close attachment to the species. You might wonder how this would be the case when they are so truly prickly. The answer comes down to their behaviour. The evolution of a spiny defence means that the hedgehog has no need of a fight or flight response. If you think about how most animals react to a perceived threat, it is with fight or flight – if you get too close, they will either try and defend themselves or they will run away. But the hedgehog does neither.

The first thing a hedgehog does is frown. When you frown, you will feel muscles on your forehead contracting, causing your skin to wrinkle. For the

hedgehog, these muscles reach all the way down to their tail, causing the spines to lift up in a jagged pattern. When a hedgehog is resting and happy, all of the spines lie flat. But when it is concerned, well, it frowns. If the concern continues, then the hedgehog employs another, and very clever, muscle called the orbicularis, which acts like a drawstring on a bag, pulling the skin into a ball. Hedgehogs can remain rolled up in a ball for hours, but usually uncurl as soon as they sense danger has passed.

We will come on to who and what present the greatest threats later, but this reaction – to curl up rather than fight or flee, means that people have the chance of seeing a hedgehog close up. I believe that this is one of the key reasons behind our strange love affair with this improbable icon. Another is that we have created, in our own back gardens, the potential for an expanse of perfect hedgehog habitats ... all we need to do is learn how to share.

You can get nose-to-nose with a wild hedgehog. This is important. The connection this gives us to a wonderful wild and sentient animal is, almost, unique. I have argued that this makes the hedgehog the most important animal on the planet – which might have been a little hyperbolic, but I still would say that hedgehogs are far more important to us than they are normally considered to be. The moment of connection opens up the possibility of forming a relationship above and beyond the usual. The importance of this was captured by the late American natural history writer, Stephen Jay Gould, when he said: 'We will not fight to save what we do not love.' I believe we need to find ways of falling in love with the natural world, first-hand rather than on a screen – and then, maybe, we will be willing to fight to protect it.

HEDGEHOGS IN NUMBERS

....

How many spines does an adult hedgehog have? 5,000–7,000

How long are hedgehog spines? 20–30mm

And what are they made of?
Keratin, the same stuff as our hair and fingernails.

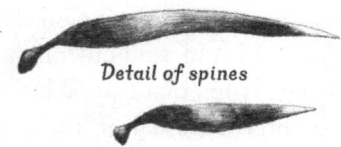

Detail of spines

How many legs does a hedgehog have? 4

Ears? 2

And does a hedgehog have a tail?
Yes, 10–20mm long.

How many young in a litter, on average? 5

How much does an adult hedgehog weigh?
Up to 1.5kg in the wild, but usually 450–800g.

How long is a hedgehog?
Although this is more theoretical as you are most likely to see them in a ball, stretched out their head and body total about 30cm.

How many hedgehogs are there in the British Isles?

A complicated question without a simple answer ... for now let's just say, there are far fewer hedgehogs than there used to be!

How many different sorts of hedgehog are there in the world?

19. Probably, though taxonomists do argue a lot!

How far can they walk in a night? 2km

How big is their home range? Up to 30ha.

How many gardens would a hedgehog visit on an average night?

This does depend a little on how big the gardens are – and how far apart. But, if you are in suburbia and you have made your garden accessible (with a 13cm hole in your fence or wall) then they can easily visit 8 gardens in one night, and often even more.

HEDGEHOG WORDS

....

What do we call a baby hedgehog?
Obviously, that is going to be a hoglet.

What about the collective noun for hedgehogs?
I got into a squabble with the organiser of a pub quiz (at a Mammal Society event, so they should have known better) for being told I was wrong with the word 'array', and that a group of hedgehogs was actually a 'prickle'. In fact, both terms are used!

Hedgehogs in trouble

. . . .

This book will look into the nooks and crannies of hedgehog life. But we must get one thing clear right from the start. Yes, hedgehogs are our favourite wild animal – and they are in serious trouble. As I've mentioned (see pages 14–15), we don't know how many hedgehogs there are in the UK (let alone in the world). The figures you may see in newspapers for the UK population are varying levels of guesswork, although researchers are working on producing a more accurate answer (see page 102).

Until we can clarify their actual number, we are relying on changes in the numbers that are seen, to try to determine how our hedgehog population is changing. This system is not perfect, but it is the best we have for now. Hold on to your hats, as we have a little bit of number-crunching to come.

Conservation bodies coordinate several national wildlife surveys that take place in the same manner each year, and respondents to these surveys can submit sightings of hedgehogs as well as other animals. So while we do not know the total number of hedgehogs in an area, this data helps us to see how their population has changed over time. These surveys are:

- 'Living with Mammals' and 'Mammals on Roads' (People's Trust for Endangered Species)
- 'Garden BirdWatch' and 'Breeding Bird Survey' (British Trust for Ornithology)
- 'National Gamebag Census' (Game & Wildlife Conservation Trust)

All the data they yield are collated, and help us generate *The State of Britain's Hedgehogs* report, updated versions of which are published every four years or so.

The latest report revealed that, since the turn of the century, hedgehog numbers in urban areas have fallen by around 25 per cent, but there is some evidence that this fall has now levelled off. The picture from the farmed landscape is less rosy. Here, the data shows a decline of between 30 and 75 per cent and, in the words of one of the authors, in some places hedgehog numbers are in complete freefall.

Why should any of this matter? Well, apart from my argument of their great importance, there is another thing to consider. Our hedgehog has the capacity to tolerate a great many different habitats. It is adaptable and robust. It's a generalist species, able to find ways to survive and thrive in many different conditions. It, or at least its closely similar ancestors, have been around on Earth in a fairly unaltered state for around 15 million years.

Yet, we are causing its numbers to plummet. And not only that, this is our favourite wild animal. Just think of all the more specialist species about which people care less. The hedgehog's decline is a massive and important warning that we would be foolish to ignore. Let's leap into a little more about the origins, habits and lives of these remarkable creatures, and then on to finding ways to help.

CHAPTER TWO

Ancient Origins and Remarkable Adaptations

If we track back through the fossil records, we find evidence from 15 million years ago of animals that had skeletons very much like those of modern hedgehogs. Whether these animals had spines is another matter, but their underlying bone structure was certainly very similar. It is not unexpected that hedgehogs have been around a while, as they are essentially glamorous shrews. And it was shrew-like animals that were the first mammals to make headway as the dinosaurs lost their dominance on land 66 million years ago.

Ancient cousins

Along the way, there have been a number of rather fascinating variations on the theme of hedgehog, within the particular shrew-like lineage that was destined to produce our familiar spiny friends. I am particularly delighted by two of these. First up is *Deinogalerix*, which lived in Italy in the Late

Miocene, 7–10 million years ago. The name translates as 'terrible shrew', and fossil evidence shows that it was three times the size of today's hedgehogs. Then there is *Exallerix manahan*, also from the Miocene, and this was a sabre-toothed hedgehog! The skull and oversized teeth show it was adapted to a life of 'hypercarnivorism', and I am very disappointed that this evolutionary line did not survive.

Taxonomy, the study of the evolutionary relationships between living things (which guides how we name species, and classify them into broader groups like families and orders), is a really useful way to get a better understanding of where animals – and plants, fungi, bacteria and viruses (though with the latter two, things are VERY complicated) – sit in the great scheme of things.

Classifying hedgehogs

So we know that hedgehogs are animals, and they are vertebrates – that is, they have a backbone. They are members of the class of mammals, like us and like our pet cats and dogs. All of us share traits such as being warm-blooded and feeding our young on milk. But then the three of us part ways. Our taxonomic order is Primates, that of the cat and dog is Carnivora, and the hedgehog's order is Eulipotyphla. Other eulipotyphlans include the shrews and moles. The name Eulipotyphla sounds dramatic, and when you translate it it's really quite insulting – it comes from the Ancient Greek for 'truly fat and blind'. However, the name is not a reference to how these animals look, but a reference to the layout of their intestines!

The next level up in taxonomic refinement is that of family, and the hedgehog's family is called Erinaceidae. As well as the hedgehogs, this family also includes the moonrats (fascinating non-prickly hedgehog-like animals from South East Asia – they are also known as gymnures, or 'hairy hedgehogs').

A family contains one or more genera (singular, genus). The family Erinaceidae contains 10 genera – five of hedgehogs and five of moonrats. Our hedgehog is classified in the genus *Erinaceus*, which is the Latin word for hedgehog. Its species name is *europaeus*, which is fairly self-explanatory.

As I have already mentioned, there are an estimated 19 species of hedgehog in the world today, spread across those five genera – though these numbers are prone to change as the taxonomists look more closely at the evidence, such as genetic differences between different populations, and rearrange things accordingly. For example, when I started hedgehogging back in 1986 there were considered to be two European hedgehog species – the Western European Hedgehog (*Erinaceus europaeus*) and the Eastern European Hedgehog (*E. concolor*). Now, though, taxonomists have split the latter into two species. There is the Southern White-breasted Hedgehog (which got to keep the name *E. concolor*), and north of the Caucasus Mountains is the Northern White-breasted Hedgehog (which has been named *E. roumanicus*).

WHAT'S IN A NAME?

What we know as a hedgehog has not always gone by that name! The first appearance of that word is from around 1450 from the Middle English *heyghoge*, which itself comes from *heyg*, meaning hedge, and *hoge* from its pig-like snout. Conveniently, it is also an animal that hogs the hedge.

As we have already seen, another name that used to be used a great deal was 'urchin'. The derivation of that word comes from the same root as the French for hedgehog, which is *hérisson*, in turn coming from the Latin, *ericius*. This name is clearly related to the hedgehog family name, Erinaceidae.

Of course there are many other names for hedgehog, see page 38 for a selection.

HOW SPECIES ARE MADE

....

The European hedgehog story is really an ice-age tale. Roll back to the Last Glacial Maximum, about 20,000 years ago, and most of northern Europe was under a thick sheet of ice. Hedgehogs didn't vanish – they tucked themselves away in warmer corners: some in Spain and Portugal, others in Italy and the Balkans. When the ice finally melted, these little survivors spread out again. The Iberian hogs headed north and west and became our familiar Western European Hedgehog. The Italian and Balkan hogs moved north and east, and over time split into two species: the Northern White-breasted Hedgehog and the Southern White-breasted Hedgehog.

That sounds neat and tidy, but it's a huge simplification. The real story is messy and fascinating and stretches far deeper into time. The last common ancestor of these three species lived about 5.8 million years ago – long before glaciers came and went. The ice didn't create hedgehogs; it just shuffled them around and nudged evolution along.

And here's a lovely twist: as Europe thawed, hedgehogs seem to have followed the spread of oak trees. It seems that both hedgehogs and oaks may well have also benefited from lifelines in the periglacial deserts provided by hot springs. So, next time you see an oak, think of hedgehogs – they have been keeping each other company for millennia.

After the last ice age, as the ice retreated, the Western European Hedgehog made its way to what is now the United Kingdom. The islands were ice-free by 11,300 years ago, and still attached to the continent until 8,200 years ago, giving hedgehogs plenty of time to cross over, spread out and fully establish themselves on mainland Britain. Hedgehogs also live on some of the islands that make up the British Isles, but we do not know how many of the islands they

NEW ZEALAND

....

The Western European Hedgehog has a range that covers, well, as the name suggests, western Europe. So how did it end up in New Zealand? We know that hedgehogs can swim, but that is quite a trek!

The story is remarkable. Back in the 1860s, colonists from England arrived in New Zealand, looked around at the great natural beauty of the islands and thought to themselves 'we need help acclimatising', and so they set up acclimatisation societies with a view to sourcing some things from home that would make them feel more, well, at home.

got to unaided, via historical natural land bridges or even (in the case of islands very near the mainland) perhaps by swimming. We do know that in at least some cases (such as the Isles of Scilly) it was people who moved hedgehogs from the mainland to the islands. How hedgehogs got to Ireland has been the subject of recent genetic research, which reveals that they may well have been brought over by the Vikings from Denmark – possibly as a food source!

And so they wrote back to England asking for hedgehogs! It was not just hedgehogs – a whole range of other animals were also introduced to New Zealand, which is why there are starlings and sparrows, rainbow trout and rabbits. Stoats, ferrets and weasels were introduced to try and control the rabbits, and conservationists have spent decades trying to undo the damage all these invasive non-native species have caused. We have to acknowledge that, despite being undeniably cute, our hedgehogs are part of the problem – eating invertebrates, lizards and birds' eggs found nowhere else on the planet. And as such, hedgehogs are being controlled by conservationists in order to save native wildlife.

Other hedgehog species

You would not fail to recognise any of the 19 (or so) species of hedgehogs as hedgehogs. They all share the same basic features – a coat of modified hair for defence, a pointy snout and a diet rich in invertebrates. They are all smallish animals, though they do vary a little in size, most of them being smaller than 'our' hedgehog. There are also some differences in spine and fur colour, but then again, there is also variation in these traits within a single species.

The most obvious way the species vary is in ear length. There are five with noticeably lengthy ears – the North African, Collared, Desert, Brandt's,

and the less imaginatively named Long-eared Hedgehog. These big-eared species all tend to inhabit hotter and drier regions so it is reasonable to assume that the size of the ears has something to do with body temperature regulation – ears are a good way to lose heat, and many other desert mammals, from Fennec Foxes to jerboas, are similarly equipped. The oversized ears of these hedgehog species are also quite mobile, so are probably important in hunting and helping to detect and pinpoint sounds more efficiently.

A HEDGEHOG CALLED HUGH

This one is, of course, personal, although the species Hugh's Hedgehog (*Mesechinus hughi*) was not actually named after me. In fact, it was a Franciscan missionary who sent a specimen back from China to London in the early part of the twentieth century – the hedgehog was identified as a new species and named after Father Hugh. I would like to meet this hedgehog – I did try a while back, but China is rather large, and Hugh's Hedgehog is really quite small.

Supersenses

· · · · · · · · · · · · · · · ·

The main sense that hedgehogs use is scent. We often hear a hedgehog snuffling along before we actually see it, and this is because a wet nose eases the transfer of scent messages to the brain (as well as making more noise as it does its sniffing). Hedgehog hearing is acute too, as anyone who has tried to take a photograph of a hedgehog with a camera that goes 'click' will know – the flinch of the hog will often blur the image. Unlike many nocturnal animals, hedgehogs do not have big eyes, suggesting sight is not very important compared to their other senses.

I was once asked an annoying question at an event by a child ... annoying in that I did not know the answer! Although I couldn't tell her at the time whether or not hedgehogs can see in colour, I took down her father's email address and sent a message when I had found out. Yes, they *can* see in colour, but not very well. Because of their lifestyle, they are primarily using their eyes after the sun has gone down, so the light-sensing cells in their retinas are mainly rods, not cones. Rods sense contrast, while cones sense colour. So rods can resolve more detail and pick up movement more readily, making them more useful at low light. Cones make up only 4 per cent of the light-sensing retinal cells, compared

Ancient Origins and Remarkable Adaptations

to 25 per cent in humans, giving hedgehogs very limited colour vision, but studies have shown that they can learn to differentiate yellow from blue, in tones that would look the same shade of grey if they were monochromatic. (I should clarify – I LOVE being asked questions, especially when I don't know the answer!)

Hedgehogs taste things, of course, and sometimes eat things they seem not to like the taste of. I watched one hedgehog that I had been radio-tracking, a male by the name of Nigel, scrabble a black slug across the surface of a quiet Devon lane, scraping off the slimy mucilage, before eating it, loudly. He then proceeded to self-anoint. More on that later.

Hedgehogs' paws appear quite dextrous, but the real indicator of their sensitivity to touch is if you gently stroke their prickles. They will flex in response. This is not a frivolous call to prod hedgehogs, but if you have found one in a nest that is very still, so still that it might in fact no longer be alive, one way to tell is to stroke the spines. Even in hibernation there will be a reaction. (Though if the hedgehog is dead, your own sense of smell will probably have already alerted you to that fact.)

Hedgehog communication

. . . .

As we have seen, the main way hedgehogs sense the world is through scent – messages about potential to mate, for example, will be spread on the breeze, and in the deposits along the way.

Apart from the rigmarole of courtship and the roughhousing of disagreements over access to a bowl of food, hedgehogs appear not to use sound a great deal. Though they can, in rare circumstances and usually associated with great stress, let out an awful scream – a pig-like squeal. This noise is alarming enough to possibly put off a potential predator.

Hoglets in the nest will sometimes make bird-like chirruping sounds – and while not 'our' hedgehog, I have heard an African hedgehog 'sing' in a hotel bedroom in Denver, Colorado.

But our understanding may be about to change as researchers have found that hedgehogs are able to hear at far higher frequencies than previously thought – sounds so high that they are beyond our ears. It is early days, but there may be an entire hedgehog world of chatter of which we are unaware!

HEDGEHOG NAMES

....

We have seen what the French for hedgehog
is, but what about the rest of the world?

Furz-pig	England
Gráinneog	Ireland
Crainneag	Scotland
Draenog	Wales
Iddy-oddy	British Isles
Pindsvin	Denmark
Igel	Germany
Egel	Holland
Igelkott	Sweden
Jeż	Poland
Yizhak	Ukraine
Ježek	Czech
Yozh	Russia
Erizo	Spain
Riccio	Italy
Siili	Finland
Kirpi	Turkey
Krimpvarkie	Afrikaans
Sündisznó	Hungary
Ežiukas	Lithuania
Cìwèi	China
Matuku	Maori

Swimming hedgehogs

. . . .

Hedgehogs might not seem the most likely animal to dive into a pool for a dip, but they can, and do, swim. Radio-tracking studies have shown hedgehogs to have crossed rivers, and Dr Pat Morris recounts how he once popped a dirty hedgehog into a lake in New Zealand and then was surprised to see it start swimming to the far side. This required the revered academic to strip down and swim out to perform a rescue. The hedgehog had been swimming for 10 minutes and was in good form by the time Dr Pat reached it. A valuable lesson was learned – yes, hedgehogs can swim well, and also, don't pop them into a lake for a bath!

The problem hedgehogs have is getting out again. This is why one of the best ways to help hedgehogs is to make sure that any water feature you might have has an escape ramp, or beach.

Now we know a bit about how the hedgehog came to be, and about its anatomy, let's look at what their life is really like.

CHAPTER THREE

A Day and Year in the Life of a Hedgehog

A 'day' in the life of a hedgehog starts as the sun goes down. Hedgehogs are nocturnal. Humans tend to be diurnal – waking from our sleep as the sun rises. There is a third pattern of activity, which is less well known – crepuscular, describing an activity pattern that has a peak at dawn and another at dusk. Being nocturnal may seem, for animals like us who rely mostly on sight to navigate the world, an odd choice. It is much easier to find your way around with your eyes. But the hedgehog is built differently and its experience of the world comes mainly through its nose and ears.

The night life

. . . .

The reasons for hedgehogs to be nocturnal are clear – their food, the macro-invertebrates (or larger creepy-crawlies if you prefer), tend to hide away during the day from the drying sun and hungry birds. As the air cools and moisture condenses into dew, they emerge to chance their luck among the hungry hogs. For a relatively slow-moving, if well-defended, mammal, night-time ambling does also give the hedgehog greater security from potential predators – though not from all the other animals of the night.

I have spent months radio-tracking hedgehogs (see illustration on page 40) as part of research to better understand their lives and improve their conservation. This has given me a very personal insight into their world and an appreciation that they all possess very individual characters. One of the things that becomes very apparent very early on in this sort of work is that generalising about almost any animal species, and certainly including hedgehogs, can be tricky! However, their individual characters are part of their charm. It is not just ecologists who notice this, but also volunteers and workers in wildlife rescue centres, who will leave advisory notes about particularly grumpy hogs for whoever is taking the next shift (or not, depending on how much they like their colleagues).

A NOTE ON BITING

I have handled hundreds of hogs but have only ever been bitten by one once. It was my fault. I was at a rescue, being interviewed by an American TV station, and they wanted me to hold the hedgehog in such a way that its face was visible. One way to do this is to pop the face between thumb and forefinger – now, have a look at your hand, and notice that thin bit of skin that connects your thumb and forefinger. And then think where the hedgehog's mouth is going to be ... like I said, my fault.

Also, this was many years ago and we have learned much more about the stress hedgehogs feel – but don't display. Reputable carers now would not do this. Hedgehogs can be filmed while being cared for, but they must not be used as playthings, nor their enclosures as petting zoos, just because they don't run away or bite (very often).

GROOMING

It may not be a question that has ever bothered you before, but I am going to make you think about it now. How does a hedgehog groom? Grooming is not just a 'nice to have', it is an essential part of life for animals. We have the advantage of opposable thumbs, combs, brushes, flannels and good plumbing, but how does a hedgehog clear away the accumulations of dirt and visitations from parasites? Especially when these things may well be found between the prickles and close to the skin.

Spend time watching a hedgehog move – I really do recommend you spend time doing this – and you may get a glimpse of legs longer than you expected. This is a good start. At the end of these legs are paws with claws that are sharp. Coupled together with a great deal of flexibility and you begin to see how a hedgehog can reach body parts that might seem inaccessible.

I have witnessed this surprising bendiness – especially when they self-anoint (page 71) – and they can reach to scratch their entire body.

Which brings up a very interesting question – what to do with hedgehogs that have lost a leg? Front leg amputees tend to be euthanised as they struggle to feed themselves. With a missing rear leg, hedgehogs can manage to walk and feed, but many rescuers now see those that have been released returning with increased parasite infestations, predominantly on the side of their body missing the rear leg, and also having an unacceptably low survival rate, leading to very difficult decisions.

When I have followed hedgehogs, they have tended mostly to time their activities with the sun (although note the earlier point about generalisations). Most will get up as the sun sets, and bed down as it rises. Hedgehogs out in the day tend to be poorly – but there will be more on what you can do about that later on. Activity peaks at the start and the end of the night, with a lull in the middle, but by 'lull', I mean just a lessening of activity – they are not heading back to bed for a snooze! Their nocturnal ways mean that hedgehog researchers have to turn their own world upside-down while working out in the field.

Getting about

Hedgehogs are very active as they work through their night shift. Normal behaviour is what you would imagine. The hog snuffles around, very much led by its nose, and moving slowly but fairly constantly. As it walks, it looks as if it is hovering just off the ground, as its legs are hidden by a skirt of prickly skin. The skirt of skin that usually hides most of the legs is crucial, as part of the wrap-around cover for when the hedgehog is rolled into a ball.

The usual pace is not brisk but a hog can reveal an impressive turn of speed when so minded. Watching a hedgehog accelerate is a delight – it seems to lift its body up, raising the 'skirt' and revealing much longer legs than you might imagine. At full stretch, a hedgehog can move at up to 9km/h, which would be a reasonable jogging pace for a human. But mostly, hedgehogs mooch, taking their time and snuffling after good things.

Hibernation

. . . .

The annual activity cycle of hedgehogs shows how unusual they truly are. The hedgehog is one of the few mammals who truly hibernates. The others in the UK are the Hazel Dormouse and all 18 species of our bats.

Hibernation is much more than a long sleep. When we humans are asleep, our metabolism is slowed down by around 15 per cent. When a hedgehog is in hibernation, this figure can be over 95 per cent. Their heart rate drops from 190 beats per minute to just 20 beats per minute, and their breathing rate falls from 20 breaths per minute to just one every two minutes. Their body temperature tends to stabilise at around 10°C, down from an active temperature of 35°C.

This very deep state of unconsciousness and profoundly slowed metabolism leaves the hedgehog vulnerable. It does not wake up when a potential threat arrives, such as a predator or a flood.

HIBERNATION RESERVES

To survive hibernation, a hedgehog needs to pile on as much fat as possible in the autumn – so it has to eat plenty of food. We can help by making sure we have not destroyed all the wild food it needs, by encouraging invertebrate life in our gardens, and we can also offer some supplementation.

Remember, hedgehogs are carnivores (meaning they eat other animals rather than plants) and need meat. The best and easiest food we can offer hedgehogs in addition to their natural diet is kitten kibble.

There are two types of stored fat. Most of it is white fat; this is the stuff that is used to keep the motor of life ticking over while the hedgehog hibernates. And then there is brown fat – this is concentrated around the chest and shoulders and these fat cells are full of mitochondria – tiny structures that convert stored fuel into energy. This could best be described as the 'starter motor'. When the hedgehog is triggered by changing temperature or disturbance, brown fat is what starts burning first, pulling the hedgehog back to consciousness. It is crucial that hedgehogs have sufficient supplies of both fat types if they are to make it through hibernation and wake up safely in spring.

One of our concerns is that warmer and wetter winters are encouraging hedgehogs to wake more frequently, depleting the vital starter motor.

In laboratory conditions, emergence from hibernation can take 2–5 hours, but in an outdoor enclosure it was recorded as around 12 hours.

Because of the significance of hibernation it makes most sense to start an account of a hedgehog's year not on January 1st but in March, with the beginning of its emergence from hibernation. Hedgehogs will sometimes be seen at other times in the winter, maybe moving to a new hibernaculum (the hibernation nest). But by March they have definitely started to come out of that long sleep and to begin the next, and vital, part of their year. And that is eating!

Hibernation is not 'cost-free'. A hibernating hedgehog is still metabolising stored food reserves, albeit at a very much reduced rate. And the more times a hedgehog is disturbed and brought to more metabolically costly wakefulness, either through warm spells of weather or our clumsiness, the more these reserves will be depleted.

Springing to life

Emerging from hibernation is a particularly vulnerable time for a hedgehog. Depleted fat reserves can leave them thin, so if you have hedgehogs in your garden, this is a good time to start to leave out some food for them.

Males tend to be the earlier risers. Studies of hedgehogs killed on the roads in spring show that around 65 per cent of them are male; by the summer this has evened out and in the autumn, more females are found. In the spring, the theory goes, the males emerge sooner so they can get a head start on looking for potential mates, as well as food, and this increased activity increases opportunities to cross roads. After mating season, though, the males' involvement in the furtherance of the species is over. So while females are working in the summer, feeding and caring for young, males can spend this time laying down fat reserves for winter, and therefore be ready to head off to hibernation earlier. Females, however, may well be left scrabbling around for food to reach a safe hibernation weight as the nights draw in, and have to travel further for food as the invertebrates begin to hide away. This, in turn, increases the chances that they will cross a road.

So the spring is a time of females eating and males searching for females, as well as eating too, of course. Now, I know I have said this before, and I will say it again, but the best thing to help feed hedgehogs is to make sure that there is natural food in your garden. Kitten kibble is only ever a supplement. Also, we must not forget drinking – the existence of accessible and safe sources of water is crucial and here, too, gardeners and landowners can help out.

THE HEDGEHOG'S YEAR

January

Hedgehogs are, hopefully, deeply secure in their hibernaculum. They will likely make use of log piles and leaves that are left in the garden.

February

Much as January, but in reality, hedgehogs have been getting up for a snoop around – sometimes they like a change of scene.

May

This is the month when romance really comes to the fore – though, to look at hedgehog courtship, it might not strike you as very romantic!

June

Babies are born – mothers work very hard to keep themselves and the little ones fed. Dads are still searching for further opportunities to mate.

September

Now is the time for hedgehogs to start thinking about fattening up. Please be careful if you are planning on tidying up, as you may be inadvertently destroying the homes of hedgehogs.

October

By now, the race is really on to lay down enough fat to see hedgehogs through hibernation – remember, they need meat. And also to find a good place to build the all important hibernation nest.

March

Shoots of spring are appearing, and hedgehogs are stretching with a view to getting up and out there with one thing on their mind – food.

April

Hedgehogs are out and about now, with two things on their minds – food and the furtherance of the species.

July

Youngsters start to be seen out of the nest – sometimes in a trail behind mum, sometimes being picked up by their scruffs to be moved to a new nest.

August

If it is a hot and dry year, make sure there is water out in shallow dishes, and keep an eye out for any hedgehogs that appear to be drunk or sunbathing.

November

Now to rest – hopefully, with some help, hedgehogs will have been able to build a hibernaculum under a log pile or behind a shrub using all the leaves that were not 'tidied away'.

December

Hedgehogs may still venture out occasionally, but mostly, they will be tucked up in something so much deeper than sleep ... I wonder if they dream?

Courtship

. . . .

During hibernation the reproductive organs of both sexes generally regress – males stop producing sperm, and in females the uterus shrinks. These spring back to life as the nights shorten. Hedgehogs are usually solitary creatures, but males are attracted to females as the females approach oestrus, the time when they are fertile. And this is when you might just witness hedgehog courtship. The great hedgehog guru, Dr Pat Morris, says of the hedgehog mating ritual, 'Courtship is a grandiose term for what is actually a rather ill-tempered and seemingly tedious affair.'

Mating cannot take place while the female frowns. And frown she will while the male begins the 'hedgehog carousel' – circling around the female, attempting to get behind her. She counters this, if it is unwanted attention, by turning on the spot so that she remains facing the male, with her head low – and delivering a sequence of distinctive plosive sneezes in his direction. So dramatic can these noises be that it is not unusual to find stories appearing in the papers of people being disturbed by what they thought were intruders, but in fact turned out to be courting hedgehogs!

Eventually she may relent – though the carousel can go on for over an hour – and will press her belly to the ground, raising up her rear end, and, most importantly, lowering her prickles into a relaxed state, allowing him to mount her. And here ends the male's involvement in the rearing of youngsters! If mating is successful, pregnancy lasts around five weeks, and the result is, on average, a litter of five babies.

HEDGEHOG BABIES

....

At birth, the hoglets are around 5cm long and
weigh 12–16g. They are born complete with
their coat of spines – which sounds alarming.
But fortunately for the mother, the spines are
concealed beneath an oedemic, fluid-filled,
layer of skin. As this fluid is absorbed into the
hoglet's body after birth, the spines emerge.
This means that the prickly defence appears
far sooner than if the spines had to start
growing at birth.

The natal nest will be their home for
much of the next four weeks or so, though
they may be taken on adventures, following
their mother. But by six weeks they are ready
for independence, and there is little evidence
of any familial association between the
siblings, nor between them and their mother,
once they have left the nest.

Raising the young

. . . .

Nesting mothers are very sensitive to disturbance and can end up abandoning or even eating their young if they really feel threatened. So please do be careful – and if you accidentally uncover a nest, re-cover it as soon as possible and leave well alone. Additionally, be aware of that spot, and if you find any youngsters out and about in the day, that could be a sign the mother has gone. If so, the youngsters can be saved, and in due course returned to the wild, if they are taken to an experienced rehabilitator. There are contacts in the back of this book for where to find help.

HOW TO AGE A HEDGEHOG

Again it was Dr Pat Morris who came up with the idea of counting growth rings, just like you do with a tree. He reasoned that while a hedgehog hibernates, it is not growing, and that when it emerges, it starts growing again. This should produce a measureable pattern in the animals' bone tissue.

He collected lots of hedgehogs that had been killed by cars and had a look at thin slices through the lower jaw bone. Here he found telltale rings, indicating the number of winters they had been through. Other researchers have since applied this method to age hedgehogs and in 2023 a Danish study produced a real surprise – a hedgehog that had lived to the age of 16!

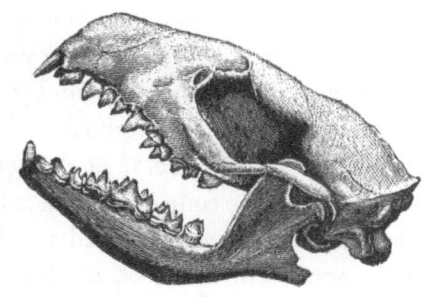

The earliest litters are born around May, but the majority are born in June and July, with later litters either being those born to mothers in their first year, when courtship may take longer, or possibly second litters from mothers that either bred early, or lost their first litter. For the newly independent hoglets, and their tired mothers too, the race is now on to ensure they put on enough weight so that when the drive to hibernate starts, they have enough fat reserves to cope.

When it comes to hedgehogs' average and potential lifespan, this is difficult to assess because most hogs live and die without ever being observed by humans. However, there are some things that we do know for certain. For example, most baby hedgehogs do not make it to their first birthday. And we have long supposed from the limited data we have on survivorship that any hedgehog that makes it to seven years old is, by the standards of its species, pretty ancient. However, some recent research suggests that the potential lifespan could be considerably longer.

After the high mortality of the first year, the annual adult mortality rate is between 20 and 30 per cent. You could look at this and just imagine it is nature taking her course, but there's no escaping the fact that many of the threats that hedgehogs face are anthropogenic – so a huge number of hedgehogs are dying as a result of human actions.

HIBERNATION WEIGHT

....

There is a lot of debate about how much a hedgehog needs to weigh if it is to survive hibernation – and because some well-meaning people care a great deal about hedgehogs, this can get quite heated. There are ways to work out at least an approximate answer. Making an educated assumption of a 30 per cent weight loss during hibernation, and then weighing the first hedgehogs you see in the spring, means you can extrapolate back to how much they would have weighed when they settled down for the winter. Based on this calculation, Dr Pat Morris

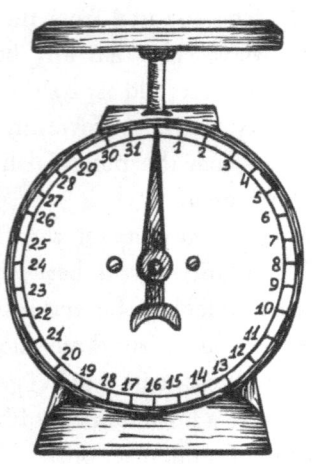

concluded that hedgehogs weighing less than 450g were not surviving the winter.

That does not necessarily mean that hedgehogs found in the autumn that do weigh well over 450g are in ideal condition. We have seen that hedgehogs need to have good reserves of fat to survive hibernation, but the problem is that weight is NOT the only measure of fitness. There can be healthy hedgehogs weighing a rather low 500g that will sail through the winter, and there can be portly hogs tipping the scales at twice that weight that are less likely to survive hibernation because they are simply not as fit.

CHAPTER FOUR

What's on the Menu?

While we may no longer have a sabre-toothed hedgehog to contend with, hedgehogs are very definitely carnivores – they catch and eat other animals. Their dentition and intestines are all evolved to cope with a diet high in animal protein. As the hedgehog snuffles through the borders of your garden, it is hard to think of it as a rapacious predator, but that is only because you are not a worm, or one of the other myriad little animals that make up the hedgehog's diet. In fact it is worth considering this – in terms of size, the hedgehog is bigger than 99 per cent of all animals that have ever lived on this planet. It is in the top 1 per cent, alongside blue whales, *Tyrannosaurus rex* and us!

Dietary composition

. . . .

If you were to spend a lot of time carefully examining the stomach contents of 137 dead hedgehogs, as the late, and wonderful, Derek Yalden did, you would probably find (as he did) that around 73 per cent of the animals represented by the remains were beetles. The next most popular items would be earwigs, caterpillars, millipedes and worms.

Of course, these days researchers have easier ways to find out what has been eaten by hedgehogs. Taking samples of hedgehog poop is one option – previously, this would have been teased apart with meticulous care and a strong stomach. Now, the DNA can be checked, and can return some rather alarming results. It took a moment for one set of researchers to work out how the hedgehog had been eating pigs and cows, until the obvious answer of pet food came to mind!

NO MILK PLEASE

....

For many years it was thought that a suitable food for a hedgehog would be bread and milk. The fact that I am asked about this in nearly every talk I give shows how deeply embedded this wrong-headed idea has become. I imagine that this ridiculous notion came, at least in part, from the sixteenth-century belief that hedgehogs threatened the nation's grain reserves, and they were also accused of stealing milk from cows' udders. So widespread was this belief that parishes paid a bounty for each hedgehog killed. (There is a fascinating and rather depressing book by Roger Lovegrove, called *Silent Fields*, that charts the killing of wildlife across England and Wales.) This was reinforced by the fact that hedgehogs would eat bread and milk, although we now know that adult hedgehogs, as with most other mammals, are lactose intolerant, and so they shouldn't consume milk! So – do not give hedgehogs milk and bread. These animals are ferocious hunters and need meat to remain healthy.

WHAT'S NO LONGER
ON THE MENU!

....

Right back to the time of Aristotle, around 2,300 years ago, there have been questions raised about what hedgehogs eat. A little later it was Pliny the Elder who wrote up some of Aristotle's ideas, and given such wise sources, these 'facts' remained uncontested for centuries.

These tales soon became a staple of hedgehog iconography, appearing in the beautiful bestiaries painted by monks and carved into the misericords of at least one chapel. However, they were simply wrong – but just like now, repetition gave them credibility.

The story was that hedgehogs would collect fruit on their spines and take this back to their burrows to store up for the winter.

You can see how the tale came about – as long as you are not a stickler for evidence. How do hedgehogs survive winter when they are not seen out and about feeding? Well, they must make a food store. What food would this be? Well, in the autumn it is not unreasonable to expect to find hedgehogs snuffling around fallen fruit, so it must be the fruit. Great, but how do they carry the fruit? Obviously they impale the fruit on their spines ...

Now we know that hedgehogs are snuffling around the fruit to eat the invertebrates attracted to that bounty. They are, in effect, collecting the calories from the fallen fruit and ferrying them back to their hibernaculum – but doing so in the form of fat.

The ancient wisdom unravels further when you discover that hedgehogs don't eat fruit, particularly. And if anyone has seen a hedgehog carrying grapes on its spines, PLEASE let me know!

I did meet a researcher who carried out an experiment with ripe plums (I think it was the sort of experiment that was concocted in a pub). He discounted the idea that hedgehogs were rolling around on fruit to collect it and generously supposed that maybe Aristotle had seen a hedgehog that had walked beneath a tree or vine from which fruit had fallen, becoming impaled on the spines. He found that, onto a walking, or happy, hedgehog, fruit will not stick. The spines are all lying flat. How about an unhappy hedgehog? Maybe that would work, but in the rare moments plums stuck, as soon as the hedgehog started to walk, they fell off.

Which leads us to the unhappy conclusion that not everything the great and ancient thinkers thought was actually true.

Unfortunate offerings

Despite their lactose intolerance, hedgehogs will seek out and avidly consume dairy products. It took the British Hedgehog Preservation Society (BHPS) eight years of hard campaigning to get fast food retailers McDonald's to change the design of their McFlurry cup. A McFlurry is, so my researchers (my children) tell me, a sort of soft ice cream-like pudding – and the hole in the top of the cup was big enough for a hedgehog to squeeze its head through. However, due to the spines, the hedgehog couldn't then withdraw its head when it had finished licking up the inappropriate contents from a discarded McFlurry cup. We knew that this had been happening because of grim discoveries of dead hedgehogs with their heads stuck in the cups.

While there is a point in that story about the design of the cup, which is relevant to other packaging too, it also serves as the reminder that hedgehogs, like humans, will eat things that are not necessarily very good for them.

There are other foods that can get some hedgehog carers into a tizzy – even though they seem much more suitable and might therefore be offered by hedgehog lovers who do know that hedgehogs are predators. However, if you regularly feed your garden hedgehog lots of mealworms, the sort you may put out for the birds, there is some evidence that this diet can cause metabolic bone disease, a thinning of the bones due to a leaching of calcium.

However, that does not mean you need to go around the bird table in the evening hoovering up any spillage for fear a hedgehog will drop down dead if it eats one or two. There needs to be a little bit of common sense when it comes to this sort of thing!

Finding prey

Watching a hedgehog hunt is fascinating. One night, while I was living in a caravan in a Devon field, radio-tracking hedgehogs, I had a brilliant opportunity to observe this close up. The hog in question was Nigel, who we have already met in chapter 2 (I had given my hedgehogs names as I was living alone in that field, and was out all night – I was watching them in lieu of any human company!). He had presented himself outside my caravan as I was getting ready to brush my teeth.

As far as I was concerned, this should have been bedtime for the both of us, as the sun was already beginning to warm the clouds. But he was there and I just popped the toothbrush in my pocket and followed him.

We have established that hedgehogs can see quite well, but their principal sense is scent. And this was very evident as I watched him being led by his nose along the edge of the narrow lane running alongside the field that was my home. If you have not had the delight of doing this, watch a dog on a walk and you'll notice how it really looks like the nose pulls them away from where they were walking.

There was risk involved in his behaviour. Nigel walked on the tarmac of the single-lane road, snaffling morsels from the damp, dew-laden grass of the verge. So he was keeping his tummy dry, but at the risk of a potential meeting with a car.

Most of the morsels were small slugs, but then he found a larger one and, as I described in chapter 2, dragged it across the tarmac, scraping off the slime, before starting to eat – which he did in a manner which suggested a degree of distaste, open-mouthed and noisy. And then he started to slap his jaws together even more, producing an excess of saliva, which he then spread across his spines with some quite extraordinary contortions. It was a classic case of self-anointing.

SELF-ANOINTING

Hedgehogs have the ability to twist their bodies around in order to groom, and this is most dramatic when they self-anoint. They will appear to be foaming at the mouth as they build up a good quantity of saliva, which they then spread across their spines. The behaviour is usually stimulated by strong scents or flavours, so possibly it is something to do with spreading that scent onto their spines, increasing its reach. However, self-anointing has also been stimulated by distilled water – so the reasons behind it remain a mystery. All the more reason to study hedgehogs in even greater depth.

HEDGEHOGS AND
BIRDS' EGGS

....

I got started in hedgehog research because they were thought to be eating the eggs of ground-nesting birds on North Ronaldsay, Orkney. They were not native to the island, and were imported in 1974 by the postman, John Tulloch, to help control garden pests. The couple he brought over proceeded to ignore the task they were set, and vanished into the ditches and fields of this tiny speck of land – just five miles long and a mile wide.

A decade later, the bird observatory noted that increased sightings of hedgehogs seemed to correspond to the failure of many ground-nesting birds to breed. My job was to find out how many there were, and to see if they were truly a threat.

They certainly can, and do, eat birds' eggs – but was it enough to explain the disappearance of birds such as the Arctic Tern? I returned a few years later to repeat the work, and it became clear that hedgehogs were part of the problem. But many other factors were also at play, such as changes in farming practices and climate change.

A very similar problem emerged on the Uists, in the Outer Hebrides. Hedgehogs introduced in the early 1970s spread widely across the islands, with declines in bird breeding success following in their wake. Research led by the RSPB highlighted the scale of the issue and, in 2003, a programme of eradication was introduced, involving the Scottish Government and NatureScot. Initially, this involved the culling of hedgehogs, which prompted significant public outcry.

Further research that I was involved in demonstrated that hedgehogs could instead be successfully live-captured and translocated to the mainland, an approach that has been adopted since 2007. A Technical Advisory Group, of which I am a member, is now helping to develop this work at scale, creating what is effectively a world-first approach to invasive species management using live capture and translocation. The law has since been changed to make it illegal to import hedgehogs onto the islands.

Feeding hedgehogs

. . . .

I am often asked which foods should be put out to help hedgehogs. There are many hedgehog foods on the market, and some of them contain ingredients that are absurd – cereals, bananas, peanuts and other vegetable matter from far-flung shores. Remember, hedgehogs are carnivores and need meat. The cheapest and easiest to find is kitten kibble.

But I also ask you to consider why you are putting out food. Is it to help hedgehogs? Or is it to increase your chances of seeing hedgehogs? Now, I am not saying it is a bad thing to want to get to see a hedgehog, but you should be aware that the

best way to help hedgehogs is to have a garden so richly abundant with invertebrates that your prickly visitors don't need any supplements.

There is some evidence that there is an increase in aggressive behaviour between hedgehogs and this is probably related to food hotspots being created in gardens. Hedgehogs are naturally solitary animals, practising a behaviour called 'mutual avoidance' – which means that, on the whole, if they simply smell another hog they will take a diversion to avoid a meeting. But if the lure of food is particularly strong from a particular place, they are more likely to come into contact. And a consequence of this is an increased number of fights.

Hedgehog fights are not life-threatening. They look and sound far worse than they are – often it will involve one hedgehog pushing into another. The attacked hedgehog will roll into a ball and can then be pushed around the place in a very strange reimagining of *Alice in Wonderland*'s croquet game (I wonder whether this is where Lewis Carroll got his idea of having Alice and the Queen of Hearts use hedgehogs as croquet balls?). Hedgehogs also can become grumpy when it comes to mating – especially if more than one male decides to try to woo a female who is coming into season.

This antisocial behaviour whenever hedgehogs meet leads to the suggestion that maybe offering just a single bowl of food in a garden is not a great idea.

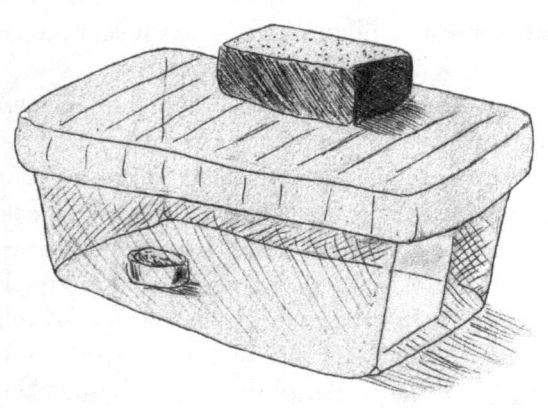

So, what is the best way to offer food to hedgehogs? The first thing to consider is how to ensure it is a hedgehog that finds the food and not a cat, rat, fox, bird or other beastie. And with that in mind, let me introduce you to the idea of a feeding station.

An upturned plastic or wooden box, with a hog-sized (13cm diameter) access hole cut into one wall, is the basic form for a suitable feeding station, and placing food in here will stop birds stealing it at dawn. Put a brick on top and that should stop a fox knocking it over. You may still have a problem with your neighbours' cats – and for these, people are getting creative as they realise how fluid cats can be. One solution is to build in a partition so that the entrance to the box becomes more of a tunnel, with the food in a dish by the front wall, requiring the hog to snuffle in and walk around. Hopefully this will be too tight a turn for a cat. As for keeping out rats, this is harder. There is some evidence that having the food in a corner reduces the amount of time a rat will spend 'trapped' under the box, as it will feel too vulnerable to linger. But it is very hard to exclude rats completely.

So much thought has already gone into designing the perfect hog feeding station – and you may have ideas of your own. It is hardly surprising that we are so motivated to take care of these animals, as they have been a part of human lives for, well, as long as civilisations have kept records of such things. The next chapter shares some of these moments.

CHAPTER FIVE

Hedgehogs and Us

As we have seen, our nation's fondness for the hedgehog is pretty intense and also near-universal. This is an animal that we mostly regard as cute, bumbling, friendly, or at the very least, harmless. It is strange, then, that for much of history and across many of the countries that fall within their natural range, that is not how hedgehogs have been seen.

Imagery from
ancient times

. . . .

The people of ancient Egypt – and those of the early civilisations of Mesopotamia and Samaria – also had a relationship with their local hedgehog species, though it is hard to understand what this meant. There are many ceramic representations of hedgehogs from those times – and one could imagine that there may have been many others made of wood, which did not survive. The nature of the imagery suggests that these peoples thought of the hedgehog as an animal that 'died' and then was reborn – not necessarily through hibernation, though, as hedgehogs of hot climates instead practise aestivation – the summer equivalent of hibernation, whereby the period of inactivity is timed to escape the worst of the heat (*hiber* from Latin meaning winter, and *aestus* referring to heat or summer).

Or maybe these civilisations were impressed by hedgehogs because they saw them as invulnerable to snakebite. Many of the most dangerous snakes of these regions – as in the ones people would bump into on a regular basis, rather than the most venomous – have fangs shorter than hedgehog spines. There is an illustration from Alfred Edmund Brehm's *Life of Animals*, published in Germany in 1895, that shows a hedgehog tackling an adder. This is certainly very rarely witnessed, and may be the result of a hedgehog bumping into a cold snake, taking advantage of the reptile's sluggishness and starting to eat.

There is also some evidence that hedgehogs have some capacity to tolerate venom from both snakes and scorpions, so maybe the artefacts are telling us of a reverence towards the hedgehog because of its resistance to these dangerous and feared animals? Maybe people hoped that the presence of a representation might help protect against attack? Of course, it is also possible that young people simply found hedgehogs cute, and that the models were just toys.

Hedgehog place names

· · · · · · · · · · · · · · · ·

The meetings of the European Hedgehog Research Group always have a far greater number of researchers from the UK than any other country. It might therefore seem odd that there is no town named 'hedgehog' in the UK, when both France and Germany have one – Herrison and Igel, respectively.

Ross-on-Wye, in Herefordshire, could claim to be the UK's 'hedgehog town'. Around 1,500 years ago, it was home to Celts and was then named Ergyng – the land of the hedgehog. I would, and I am sure you would too, take this name as a compliment to the town – but I do wonder whether it was actually designed as an insult, considering that (as we will see later) the Celtic word for hedgehog translates as 'ugly one'.

Although the town's present-day name has no obvious connection to hedgehogs, local records show how, over the centuries, hedgehogs were in evidence. In 915 the Anglo-Saxon Chronicle referred to Ircingafeld, in 1086 the Domesday Books gives us Arcenfelde, and by 1679 this had changed to Urchenfeld, another link to hedgehogs – or 'urchins'! If you are ever in Ross-on-Wye, be sure to visit St Mary's Church, which has at least 14 images of hedgehogs to find.

Picture books and poetry

Hedgehogs' public image received a tremendous boost after October 1905 when the brilliant English scientist and illustrator, Beatrix Potter, published her much-loved hedgehog story, *The Tale of Mrs Tiggy-Winkle*. Since then, hedgehogs have appeared in numerous UK-based stories for children. The long list includes the *Percy the Park Keeper* books by Nick Butterworth; Dick King-Smith's *The Hodgeheg*; *Fuzzypeg Goes to School* by Alison Uttley; *Hogarth Peel: The Space-Travelling Hedgehog* by Ted MacKenzie; *Princess Kalina and the Hedgehog* by Jeannette B. Flot; and Richard Mayers's *Spikez* books, featuring a cyborg hedgehog.

Prickly Poems, published in association with the BHPS, reminds us that it is not just folk tales and childrens' stories that have been inspired by our spiny neighbour. John Clare's poem *The Hedgehog* begins with these lines:

The hedgehog hides beneath the rotten hedge
And makes a great round nest of grass and sedge
Or in a bush or in a hollow tree
And many often stoop and say they see
Him roll and fill his prickles full of crabs
And creep away and where the magpie dabs
His wing at muddy dyke in aged root
He makes a nest and fills it full of fruit ...

We do need to unpick that a little. The 'crabs' here are crab apples, not crustaceans – and hedgehogs don't actually collect fruit and store it!

The late and very great Benjamin Zephaniah gifted us the poem *Luv Song*.

I am in luv wid a hedgehog
I've never felt this way before
I have luv fe dis hedgehog
An everyday I lov her more an more,
She lives by de shed
Where weeds and roses bed
An I just want de world to know
She makes me glow.

I am in luv wid a hedgehog
She's making me hair stand on edge,
So in luv wid dis hedgehog
An her friends
Who all live in de hedge
She visits me late
An eats off Danny's plate
But Danny's a cool tabby cat
He leaves it at dat.

I am in luv wid a hedgehog,
She's gone away so I must wait
But I do miss my hedgehog
Everytime she goes to hibernate.

But perhaps my favourite prickly poem comes from the inimitable Pam Ayres. *The Last Hedgehog* is not only heart-wrenching and sad, but also full of all the top tips you can undertake to make sure we don't end up with the last hedgehog.

> From now on, as you pull the drapes
> You'll see no round familiar shapes,
> Nevermore from dusk till dawn
> Will we eat slugs on your lawn,
> So little gratitude you've shown
> From now on you can eat your own.

It is the animal that keeps on giving – even as children have been lured away from the magical world of books, the hedgehog is still there, centre stage in a certain computer game and film franchise (see pages 90–91).

Fairy tales and fables

Early stories of hedgehogs reveal that they were regarded as animals of portent, and the future they indicated was often doom-laden. The Brothers Grimm story *Hans My Hedgehog* is, in its original form, deeply disturbing, featuring the birth of a half-human, half-hedgehog child, who goes on to use trickery to marry a princess (and badly injure another).

Earlier hedgehogs, though, had the potential to inspire philosophical murmurings. The ancient Greek poet Archilochus said, 'The fox knows many things, the hedgehog knows just one, good thing.' This idea about the clever fox and wise hedgehog was reprised in the twentieth century by the philosopher Isaiah Berlin, in his famous long-form essay *The Hedgehog and the Fox*, published in 1953. Here Berlin takes the ancient idea and spins it out into an entire vision of looking at thinkers. There are those he describes as foxes, who draw on a wide range of ideas through which to see the world, and then there are hedgehogs, who view the world through the lens of a single defining idea. (I have personally become a philosophical hedgehog, who thinks and knows about hedgehogs!) Folk tales from Africa feature the jackal and the hedgehog in much the same sort of relationship.

Shakespearean hedgehogs

. . . .

It is hard to imagine, given the affection with which we regard hedgehogs today, that they were not always so beloved. However, the works of Shakespeare reveal that the late sixteenth-century view of hedgehogs was none too fond. For example, in *Richard III*, Act 1, Scene 2, the name 'hedgehog' is used as an insult:

> Dost grant me, hedgehog? Then, God grant
> me too
> Thou mayst be damned for that wicked deed!
> O, he was gentle, mild and virtuous!

In *A Midsummer Night's Dream*, Act 2, Scene 3, hedgehogs are listed among the other low beasts:

> You spotted snakes with doubt tongue,
> Thorny hedgehogs be not see;
> Newts and blinders, do no wrong,
> Come not near our fairy queen.

So why was the hedgehog a term of insult? In Welsh, Gaelic and Scottish its names are *draenog, gráinneog* and *gràineag*, respectively – all words that translate to something like 'the ugly one'. Clearly the references from Shakespeare allude to something similar.

Commercial hedgehogs

The fondness for hedgehogs that pervades society has not gone unnoticed by brand advertisers. Hedgehogs spring up in the most unlikely of places. A few British pubs are named after hedgehogs, as are various beers and ciders – and the Côtes du Rhône Villages wine appellation used a hedgehog in their advertising for a few years.

If you look through the cleaning aisle of your supermarket, you may find scrubbing brushes branded with hedgehogs. A French TV advert from Spontex, makers of sponges, featured a hedgehog becoming captivated (in a rather inappropriate manner) with a particularly seductive scouring pad.

The Department for Transport in the UK used hedgehogs in road safety films targeted at children in a 1990s campaign ... despite the fact that children were more likely to see a hedgehog squashed dead on the road than alive. When I mentioned this to a DfT official, they admitted the success of the campaign was, at least in part, measured in how much children loved the stickers! The fact that Goodyear has used hedgehogs in their advertisements for car tyres is, I think, in poor taste.

HEDGEHOG SUPERSTARS

······················

It pains me deeply that when I talk in schools
I find students tend to have spent far more time
in the company of Sonic the Hedgehog than
they have with a real one. The bright blue heroic
hedgehog of numerous video games (as well as
films and television programmes) doesn't have
much in common with a real hedgehog, although
he can roll into a ball at will, enabling him to
travel even faster than his usual running pace
and smash through obstacles as well. When the
original Sonic game was first being developed

by Sega, back in the late 1980s, they initially wanted to use a rabbit as the fast-running hero. But to make the rabbit work, they wanted its ears to flap as it ran, and this was too difficult to programme for the tech available at the time, so the developers looked instead for an animal with external bits that did not flap, and landed on the hedgehog.

Hedgehogs as pets

. . . .

I have quite strong feelings on this subject. Firstly, and this must be made very clear right at the outset, 'our' hedgehog, the Western European Hedgehog, is never going to make a good pet. However, since the early 1990s, when an exotic pet dealer from the USA was making a visit to Africa and spotted some hedgehogs in a cage, interest in pet hedgehogs has grown. The two species most often kept are the Southern African Hedgehog (*Atelerix frontalis*) and the Four-toed Hedgehog (*Atelerix albiventris*), often collectively called 'African pygmy hedgehogs'. They are, indeed, smaller than our hedgehog. They also tend to live in drier environments, with adaptations including drier (and less smelly) faeces.

The initial flurry of fascination for pet hedgehogs eased off, but not before there was a brief spell when selling them was making some people good money. Then supply dried up as their import was banned – which led to some unsophisticated breeding, creating rather linear family trees and with it the emergence of an unpleasant inherited condition, Wobbly Hedgehog Syndrome.

In the USA there are no wild hedgehogs, but here in the UK we have our own hedgehog. This creates a problem when pet hedgehogs capture positive publicity, sparking demand ... and every now and

then there are photographs in the tabloids of baby pet hedgehogs looking utterly cute.

If pet hedgehogs became much sought-after in the UK, two things would happen. Firstly, unscrupulous folk would start trying to flog native wild hedgehogs as pets – this would be cruel to the animals and also unfair on anyone buying them. Secondly, even legitimate pet hedgehogs don't make great pets. They are nocturnal, need to run on a wheel at night, and will often poop in their wheel, resulting in a shower of faecal material which needs to be cleaned from between their spines. Consequently, some unhappy owners would dump their unwanted pets in the wild – perhaps reasoning that, after all, there are hedgehogs living out there already, so what is the worry?

Sometimes, a non-native species thrives and becomes hugely problematic. Released African hedgehogs, though, are not going to start breeding in the wild in the UK, nor interbreeding with native hedgehogs. They will simply die in our climate, as they need constant warmth. The luckiest may be taken to a wildlife rescue – but they cannot release them, so they are burdened with another mouth to feed.

FUN AND GAMES

Pet hedgehogs are still popular in the USA. Associated events include the Rocky Mountain Hedgehog Show, which I visited one year, and the International Hedgehog Olympic Games. This is more of a triathlon than a full-blown array of sports, consisting of the sprint – hedgehogs racing along a track in a large hamster ball; the hurdles, where they are encouraged to race over obstacles; and finally the floor exercises, wherein the hedgehog must go through a tunnel, over a see-saw, and, for reasons that nobody could explain to me, knock over a 'My Little Pony'. The first two events are timed, and the floor exercises are scored based on the stylishness of the performance.

FLEAS

....

One of those things many of us have heard about hedgehogs is that they are covered in fleas. But are they really? I have handled hundreds, and hardly ever seen a flea. Also, the fleas that they do have pose no risk to cats, or dogs, or us. The Hedgehog Flea – *Archaeopsylla erinacei* – is species-specific; it can only live on a hedgehog. To do so, this flea has had to evolve in such a way as to be able to cope with the very unusual environment on the back of a hedgehog. And the reason we have this story of flea-ridden hedgehogs is, I believe, because of observations of hedgehogs seen out in the daytime – because for most of our own species' history we have had limited artificial light so were less likely to see this nocturnal mammal. As most of us know, hedgehogs that are out in the day tend to be poorly. And poorly hedgehogs tend to have more parasites, including fleas, on the outsides of their bodies, as well as all sorts of nematodes (parasitic worms) and other internal parasites.

CHAPTER SIX

How to Help Hedgehogs

We know that hedgehogs in the UK are in big trouble. Why is this happening, and, more importantly, what can we do about it? For the solutions, you will have to wait a bit. First, let's look at some of the problems our hedgehogs are facing. The main threats are loss of food, loss of habitat, and the fragmentation of remaining habitat. Let's start with the issue of fragmentation, and bring that right home, into our own gardens.

Patchy problems

. . . .

The perfect habitat of a hedgehog is – well, the clue is in the name. However, hedgerows are themselves anthropogenic versions of the hog's true natural habitat, which is woodland edge. There is simply more hedge than edge these days. These habitats are crucial, providing corridor, larder and accommodation – and their absence, and degradation, in the farmed landscape is all too clear to see.

But back to our patch – the garden. If you are reading this book you probably already love wildlife (though if you are not already a fan, and you are reading, I really hope that by the end you become a convert!). As a wildlife fan you have probably already set up your garden to give nature a helping hand. Bird feeders, water in shallow dishes and perhaps a pond, planting for insects to pollinate – and you probably have noticed the birds, bats, and butterflies, moths and other flying insects that make use of it all.

The problem, from the perspective of a hedgehog, is the word 'flying'. They are, as yet, unable to use that technique for overcoming boundaries! The fences and walls that separate one garden from the next are only part of the fragmentation problem. Busy roads, canals, industrial fencing – all of these can stop hedgehogs moving. And they really need to

move – males travel on average 2km a night, females about half that.

There is also the issue of how much habitat they need to support a minimum viable population. This is a thought experiment – which can be turned into a computer model. What are the minimum requirements for a population of hedgehogs to be sustained, and able to thrive?

We can look at extremes and that might help explain. One male hedgehog on an island that is perfect will not found a viable population. A thousand hedgehogs of both sexes on a desert island with no food will not found a viable population. It turns out that in excellent habitat, the minimum viable self-sustaining population is about 30 hedgehogs, and they need nearly a square kilometre of habitat in order to thrive. Now we need to look at where we are hoping to find hedgehogs, and often we will find that it is this that is the problem; there is simply not a large enough area for them to do all those vital hedgehoggy things – find enough food to eat, water when they need it, safe shelter and potential mates.

The same problem besets hedgehogs in the farmed landscape. But here the problems are even worse, so they need a larger area and starting number as well. The farmed landscape has issues of a different order. The fragmentation has taken place over decades, as hedges were removed and those that remain are largely neglected. But the real

issue is food. Hedgehogs eat invertebrates. Many invertebrates are competitors with farmers for the crops they are trying to grow, for the consumption by humans but also livestock.

It is entirely reasonable for a farmer trying to make a profit to tackle the competition. Unfortunately, a farmer's competitors are a hedgehog's food. These invertebrates also feed farmland birds, bats, amphibians and reptiles – all of which are suffering. So this lack of food not only directly impacts hedgehogs, but also further fragments the land, as there is no incentive to start snuffling off into what is, to all intents and purposes, an ecological desert.

COUNTING HEDGEHOGS

....

The first hedgehog research I did was on the island of North Ronaldsay, where hogs had been introduced in 1974, and were having an impact on the breeding success of ground-nesting birds. This island, the most northerly in Orkney, has no trees or cliffs, and all the birds that breed there are ground-nesters.

My method was fairly crude. I marked each hog I found with a unique code – in dabs of emulsion paint carefully applied to the spines. #1 – left shoulder yellow, #2 – right shoulder yellow, and so on, which with different colours gave me plenty of options. Over time the proportion of hedgehogs I found per night without paint decreased and the proportion that I'd already marked increased. This is the heart of a technique known as 'mark, release, recapture' (MRR). I put the numbers into a big table and spent a long time making calculations (this was before I could ask a computer to do it for me) and got an answer ... that one small island had more than 500 hedgehogs.

Surveys

. . . .

My data for North Ronaldsay's hedgehog population can't be scaled up to calculate the number for the whole country, because different habitat types support different population densities. However, if we want to undertake good conservation work, knowing how many hedgehogs there are, nationally as well as regionally, is important.

We have the National Hedgehog Monitoring Programme – NHMP – which is working on that very question. This large-scale study is using a far more sophisticated technique than MRR, with arrays of wildlife cameras out generating loads of data. Initially, the video clips are fed into an online database, and then onto another platform where Artificial Intelligence removes the videos that are blank or that contain people. That should leave only clips containing animals – and AI is doing a fair job at working out what they are, but is not good enough. So that is why we need people to look at the millions (yes, millions) of short videos and help identify what is seen. And then ... well, to be honest, there I fall down. I have no idea how it works, only that very clever people have shown that it works. At one conference I asked the person who set up the project how it worked and he described it as 'statistical jiggery-pokery', which told me an awful lot!

WHO EATS HEDGEHOGS?

If it were not for those protective prickles, a lot
of predators would catch and feast on hedgehogs.
The spines do a good job on stopping most, but
there are still three predators in the UK who
have been known to eat hedgehogs. These are:
humans ... yes, hedgehogs were a part of the diet
of many rural, and most famously, travelling folk;
Eurasian Eagle-owls – of which we have very
few in the UK; and badgers.

The badger/hedgehog story is one that needs
some clarity, as there is a knee-jerk tendency
towards an ecologically unsophisticated point of
view. Badgers can and do eat hedgehogs. I have
seen it happen. Badger claws are longer than
hedgehog spines, and badgers are very strong, so
can simply pull open a rolled-up hedgehog. When
you map the presence of badgers and hedgehogs
you find that where there are most badgers, you
have very few hedgehogs, and where you have

most hedgehogs, you have very few or no badgers.

You see how easy it is to jump to a conclusion? But ecology is rarely that simple. Hedgehogs and badgers have what is known as an asymmetric intraguild predatory relationship. Most of the time they are competitors for the same food resources, which means in ecology terms that they are in the same ecological guild. However, when the wider ecosystem becomes degraded that relationship shifts, intensifying from being one of competition to one of predation. And we know which way that is going to go!

As well as being able to prey on hedgehogs, badgers have a number of key advantages that enable them to outcompete the hogs as well. When it comes to worms and other underground-dwelling invertebrates, they are simply better at hunting them, as they can dig, while hedgehogs just scratch the surface. Badgers are also more omnivorous, so can fatten up on maize, for example, when it is available.

A further negative for the hedgehog is that badgers create a landscape of fear – meaning that when a hedgehog pootles along a hedgerow and comes across a badger latrine or sett, it will take a sniff and then retreat. This shuts off exploratory options, and fragments hedgehogs' landscapes even more.

HEDGEHOG
HIGHWAY

PLEASE KEEP THIS HOLE OPEN!

www.HEDGEHOGSTREET.ORG

Creating hedgehog highways

. . . .

There are two main ways that you can help hedge-hogs. Firstly, we can make our shared environment safe, and rich in food – and this will reduce the need for the second, which is rescuing and rehabilitating individual hedgehogs. As prevention is better than cure, let's first look at ways of reducing the need to rescue hedgehogs.

We have established their basic needs – food, water, shelter, and a chance to mate. The Hedgehog Street campaign, run by the BHPS and People's Trust for Endangered Species, has produced a simple guide of top tips to help ensure those needs are met. These are aimed at our gardens (although it would be amazing if we could encourage the wider farmed and built environment to be better managed for wildlife, too, and we can make a difference through lobbying our representatives at every level).

When it comes to your garden, remember that first of all hedgehogs need to be able to get in. However wonderful your garden is, if there is no access opening at ground level, they will stick to your neighbour's garden. We have found that all that's needed is a hole, 13 x 13cm (about the size of a CD case), in the base of the fence or wall.

Obviously, this works best on a large scale, and this is probably the hardest part of Hedgehog Street.

You need to get to know your neighbours well enough to ask – not only about making a hole between their garden and yours, but also (ideally) having them extend the highway into their neighbour's garden, and so on. There are more than 100,000 hedgehog champions signed up on the Hedgehog Street campaign and many thousands have registered their hedgehog highways on the Big Hedgehog Map – where you can also record sightings.

Building a safe haven

After sorting out the access, what are the next priorities? If you are into wildlife you probably already have a pond. Ponds are amazing, and not just for birds and mammals to drink and for amphibians to breed. They also draw in invertebrates, so crucial to the function of an ecologically balanced garden. BUT – your pond needs to be designed for wildlife. Some ornamental ponds are potential deathtraps for hedgehogs. Hedgehogs can swim, but not forever. They need to be able to get out.

A wildlife pond should have a 'beach', a shallow section which enables animals to come to the water to drink safely, and also enables any that have fallen in to reach dry land. If your pond does not have such a feature, then you can create it with some stones, or even a ramp.

Third on the list is a real need to destroy the 'Cult of Tidiness'. OK, I have made up the cult, but gardeners can get swept up into the idea that neatness and order are what make a 'good' garden. They watch television programmes and read magazines celebrating gardens that are effectively ecological wastelands, where everything is controlled and nothing grows without written permission, in triplicate and countersigned by the Mayor.

If you don't want to go full wilderness (and you may want to use your garden for other things besides encouraging wildlife), how about leaving at least some of the space to go wild? Find a corner and leave it be, let it discover for itself which plants want to grow, and don't cut it back come the winter. Brambles and nettles are very good things; in fact, Hedgehog Street planted them in their show garden at the Hampton Court Palace Royal Horticultural Show one year, and won two prizes for their highly hedgehog-friendly garden.

Treacherous traps

The spines on the back of a happy hedgehog lie flat, which means it can push through holes and squeeze into places that are really quite snug. But this all goes wrong if the hedgehog has to reverse out – the spines snag and can leave the animal trapped. For this reason, litter can be deadly to hedgehogs – remember, it took a long campaign from the BHPS before the design of the McFlurry cup was changed, but this would never have been needed if people did not drop litter.

Crisp packets, drink can rings, elastic bands and sports field netting also are common offenders, and even netting around fruit in our gardens can result in tragedy. Hedgehogs get caught, and when they bristle in response to the indignity of the capture, they become further tangled. This, in itself, is a

FLYSTRIKE

Flystrike is something all wildlife rescuers fear. This is when flies lay their eggs on an animal that is already enfeebled or restrained – for example, when stuck in netting. The flies particularly lay their eggs around the soft and moist parts of the body, including any open wounds. Very soon (especially in warm weather) the eggs hatch – into maggots, which do what maggots have to do to survive, and start to eat.

I have been in a hedgehog hospital when helpers were desperately trying to remove all the eggs, clumped together around the face and rear end of a poor hedgehog. Often the hog is already weakened by the time the flies arrive, meaning it is not rolled into a tight ball. The carers I saw were using old donated dental equipment to help the hedgehog – the fine pointed tweezers were just what was needed to carefully pluck eggs from up the hog's nose, inside the ears and around the eyes.

problem, leaving them vulnerable to predators, dehydration, starvation, or worse.

Netting left on or in contact with the ground becomes a tangle hazard. If it can be replaced with something rigid, that is much better. Keeping it very taut also reduces the chances of entanglement.

An additional garden hazard was pointed out to me by a very sad friend who had found that the electric fencing around her chickens had killed two hedgehogs. As they tried to get in among the chickens (poultry manure attracts all sorts of gorgeous grubs), the hogs clambered over the fence and were given a shock, which caused them to roll around the wire. Repeated shocks kept the hedgehog in place. One probably died from dehydration but the other had been hit by flies.

The hedgehog restaurant

Something you can do to help hedgehogs is to provide food and water. A shallow dish of water is a vital component of any wildlife-friendly garden, especially those without a pond. I had tended to not to suggest this as a main feature until someone sent me a video of a hog toddling along a path at night, reaching water and then drinking for two minutes, solidly. Remember, if you do have a pond, make sure that it is safely accessible.

Food can be a little more complicated. As you already know, some of the food mixes that are marketed to hedgehog lovers are really not very appropriate for a carnivore. Wildlife food is not regulated, which is a shame. What is regulated, though, is pet food. And kitten kibble has to be very high in meat protein – so this is the food of choice of many hedgehog hospitals around the country.

HEDGEHOGS ON FILM

We can learn so much about hedgehogs from trail cameras – not only are they being used to help discover population estimates (see page 103), but they also provide insights into behaviour. There are many different cameras out there, with a wide range in price. This is not the place to list them all, but I would suggest you find a local wildlife group where enthusiasts will likely have done the research for you. The easiest way to see hedgehogs is to point the camera at the feeding station; if you are not sure whether it is hedgehogs snaffling the kitten kibble, this will provide the answer. Then share your findings – let's flood the internet with hedgehogs (far more interesting than cats!).

Don't poison the buffet!

Ecocides are chemicals used in the garden to kill or control species that are not wanted by the gardener. Lawn treatments reduce worm numbers ... but what do hedgehogs love to eat? Worms! Insecticides kill ... well, the name gives that away. And what else do hedgehogs love to eat? Insects. And on it goes. As we try to control our garden and mould it into an extension of our indoor space, we can start damaging its ecological balance.

Slugs, for example, are hated by growers of all kinds of plants, and so many gardeners turn to poisons to reduce slug numbers. The most toxic domestic slug killers have been banned, but still it is worth remembering that more than half of all slug species are specifically detritivores – their role in life is to turn dead vegetation into soil (that in turn will nourish new plants).

Hedgehogs eat slugs. Admittedly, I do get sent images of a hedgehog and a slug feeding at the same food dish, typically with a grumpy comment: 'I thought you said they ate slugs!' Well, they do, but they tend to only eat the very small ones, ones that you probably don't notice, which are often under the surface of the soil. The bigger slugs are not such tasty morsels, covered as they are in protective slimy mucus. However, many little slugs are eaten by hedgehogs before they have the chance to grow into big slugs.

The nematodes that cause hedgehog lungworm infection have slugs in their life cycle – hedgehog poop contains the nematode eggs, which get picked up by slugs, which are in turn eaten by hedgehogs. This has caused some people to think that more slugs is in some way going to lead to bigger lungworm issues, and to say that we should control slugs to protect hedgehogs. However, all of the species involved in this cycle have evolved together in balance, over the millennia.

In fact, one technique for assessing whether hedgehogs live in an area was based around this very relationship. It can be tricky or expensive to have people out over many nights looking for hedgehogs. But slugs, they are very easy to find. And can be lured to traps to drown in beer. These slugs – and this bit is yucky, so I hope you are not eating breakfast – can then be minced and the remaining gloop analysed for the DNA of the nematodes. Because you can't have slugs with these specific hedgehog-infecting nematodes without hedgehogs.

HELPING HEDGEHOGS

....

Here are ten things you can do to help
hedgehogs, from the Hedgehog Street
campaign.

Get your garden ready for hedgehogs:

1   Link your gardens with Hedgehog
    Highways.
2   Create a wild corner.
3   Leave out food and water.
4   Make a home for hedgehogs.

Look out for hazards:

5   Make ponds safe with a ramp.
6   Deal with litter and netting.
7   Stop using chemicals.
8   Check before trimming or mowing.
9   Take care with bonfires.

And finally, get others involved too:

10 Spread the word with family, friends
    and neighbours.

Garden management

Strimmers and mowers make garden work so much easier – even the scythe that I use to clear around the fruit trees in the three allotment plots I share with friends is a labour-saving device. But all of them can be lethal for hedgehogs.

Earlier on we established that hedgehogs have no fight or flight response to threats. They frown and then they roll into a ball. This is great for many problems, but not blades. Every year hedgehog rescuers get gruesome reminders of the efficiency of these tools, as they deal with casualties brought in with horrible injuries. Please, if you are going to strim, mow or even scythe, check first – the most likely place a hedgehog will be is in and around a hedge or a border, so run the blunt end of a rake through the areas you want to control, and check no one is about to get hurt.

A similar problem comes in the form of bonfires. Every autumn I spend a lot of time talking to the media, reminding people of this potential risk to hedgehogs. If you wanted to build the perfect hedgehog hibernaculum, you would collect a load of dried leaves, then you would surround these leaves with twigs. To those twigs you would then add some larger sticks, then branches and ... hey presto, you have built a hibernaculum, but unfortunately in your eyes what you have built is a bonfire. A hedgehog has no way of knowing this, of course, and as far as it's concerned you have just generously supplied it with a home. And when the fire is lit, well, you know what the hedgehog will do. It will frown and then roll into a ball, to wait until the bad thing has gone away.

There is a very simple way to prevent this tragedy from unfolding. Never build your bonfire the day before you intend to burn it. Only ever build it the day it will be lit, as this will stop nocturnal animals finding it and making themselves comfortable.

Shelter and security

The final direct hedgehog helping tip is to give them a home. Now, there is a part of me that thinks this should be redundant, because you will have already made your garden so completely inviting to hedgehogs that a separate home is not necessary – everything's there for them to find a perfect shelter for themselves. Nevertheless, it is useful to think about this, especially if you don't already have a log pile or a bank of brambles.

More than 4,300 people responded to a request from the Hedgehog Street team for information about whether their purpose-built hedgehog houses were being used. To avoid disturbance, they could use a trail camera to check who was home. An alternative was to prop a twig up in the entrance ... if it is knocked into the house, someone has visited, and if it is knocked out, someone was already home.

The results surprised me. The project – the Hedgehog Housing Census – revealed that 81 per cent of hedgehog houses had been used for day nests, 28 per cent for breeding, and 57 per cent for hibernation. The features of the garden that encouraged use were: age of the house; connectivity to neighbouring gardens; provision of food; and presence of other nesting possibilities. If your garden has all of these, there is a good chance that your hedgehog house will attract a resident. Place it with its entrance pointing into shelter,

and leave some suitable bedding material around it, such as leaves and grass.

However, it is also possible that the survey was telling us about the sort of people who already had hedgehogs in their gardens, and were then motivated to place a house there – so I would not comment on the presence of a hedgehog home as a lure.

SIGNS THAT A HEDGEHOG NEEDS HELP

The following pages explain what to do if you spot any of these signs of distress in a hedgehog:

Lethargic – hedgehogs don't sunbathe!
Flies – urgent attention is needed if there are lots of flies around it.
Wobbly – if they wobble as they walk, something is wrong.
Trapped – hogs can get stuck in netting, ponds, drains and litter.
Hoglets – baby hedgehogs need help if you see them out in the day with no adults, and/or they are squawking.
Injury – if the hog is wounded or in distress, please act.

Emergency!

. . . .

What should you do if you come across a sick or injured hedgehog, whether in your garden or in the wider countryside? Of all the wild animals in the UK, the hedgehog is the most frequently taken to wildlife hospitals. This could be seen as a positive ... that there are lots of hedgehogs to rescue, or that there are lots of people who care. Or it could be telling us that hedgehogs are in more trouble than most. In any case, their size and behaviour make intervention relatively easy, compared to larger, fiercer or more flighty animals.

How to Help Hedgehogs

HEDGEHOG FIRST AID

....

The most important thing to do if you find a sick or injured hedgehog is to get it safe and secure, as long as you can do that without endangering yourself. Here is the BHPS's advice:

If you have found a hedgehog you are concerned about, please use gardening gloves or a folded towel to collect it up. Bring it indoors and put it in a high-sided box with an old towel or fleece in the bottom for the hedgehog to hide under. Fill a hot water bottle so that when it is wrapped in a towel there is a nice gentle heat coming through, and put that in the bottom of the box with the hedgehog, ensuring it has room to get off the bottle should it get too warm. Make sure the bottle is always kept warm (if allowed to go cold it will chill the hedgehog and do more harm than good). During particularly hot weather, providing heat may not be necessary. Put the box somewhere quiet. Offer meaty cat or dog food and fresh water, then call the BHPS as soon as possible on 01584 890 801 for further advice and the numbers of local independent rehabilitators.

Because hedgehogs allow us to get close, we are able to help them. This closeness brings about a deeper connection to hedgehogs, and with that a willingness to take care of them. This feeds back into increasing the chances of our seeing them, and hopefully learning as we do that to help one species (even this exceptionally charming and fascinating species) in isolation is not enough. We need to look at the web of life, the ecosystem we all share, and learn how best to make it work for all life on Earth.

Further Reading and Resources

Clearly it is impossible to cram all that there is to know about these fascinating creatures into this one small book – so, if you are interested in digging a little deeper into the lives and habits of our favourite garden snufflers, here are some other resources that might help.

It would be foolish of me not to mention that I have written about hedgehogs before, and to invite you to check out *Hedgehog* (Reaktion, 2014), *A Prickly Affair* (Penguin, 2018) and *The Hedgehog Book* (Graffeg, 2020).

Organisations

If you find a sick or injured hedgehog, and you do not have contact details for a local wildlife rescue, get in touch with BHPS (see opposite). They have a 24-hour phone line and will get you connected to someone who can help.

The British Hedgehog Preservation Society (BHPS) – britishhedgehogs.org.uk
01584 890 801
Hedgehog House, Dhustone, Ludlow, Shropshire, SY8 3PL

The People's Trust for Endangered Species – ptes.org
3 Cloisters House, 8 Battersea Park Road, London, SW8 4BG

Hedgehog Street Campaign – hedgehogstreet.org

Prickles and Paws, Newquay, Cornwall – pricklesandpaws.org
07926 576164

Shepreth Hedgehog Hospital – swccharity.org/about-the-hospital
07947 361187
Shepreth Wildlife Park, Station Road, Shepreth, Cambridgeshire, SG8 6PZ

Vale Wildlife Hospital & Rehabilitation Centre – valewildlife.org.uk
01386 882 288
Station Road, Beckford, Nr Tewkesbury, Gloucestershire, GL20 7AN

Acknowledgements

After my initial foray into hedgehog research, Dr Pat Morris recruited me to work with him. This was the turning point of my life, where he introduced me to Roz Kidman Cox, editor of *BBC Wildlife* magazine, who in turn asked me to write a feature – the first writing I had ever done beyond letters, essays and reports. So it is with great thanks to these two kind and generous people – as without them, I would have not written this book – or be doing the work that I love.

Image Credits

All internal illustrations © Marianne Taylor, with the following exceptions: **PP 28–29:** (background) Archiwiz/ Shutterstock; **P 29:** Anastasia Lembrik/Shutterstock; **P 38:** Romry; **PP 44–45:** Topu khan/Shutterstock; **PP 48–49:** (background) daboost/iStock; **P 56:** (background) Green angel/Shutterstock; **P 58:** Morphart Creation/Shutterstock; **P 60:** LiiaLonnArt/Shutterstock; **P 64:** (top) frozenbunn/ Shutterstock, (middle) Arthur Balitskii/Shutterstock, (bottom) Yevheniia Lytvynovych/ Shutterstock; **PP 66–67:** (background) daboost/iStock; **PP 72–73:** Green angel/Shutter-stock; **P 73:** Mariia Mazaeva/Shutterstock; **P 87:** Otto Ubbelohde; **PP 90–91:** (background) Ulimi/Shutterstock; **P 95:** mart/Shutterstock; **PP 100–101:** first vector trend/ Shutterstock; **PP 104–105:** (background) Archiwiz/ Shutterstock; **P 104:** Bodor Tivadar; **P 111:** (background) Dolka/Shutterstock, (flies) PackagingMonster/Shutterstock; **P 114:** Morphart Creation/Shutterstock; **P 116:** daboost/ iStock; **P 122:** Mr Twister/Shutterstock.

Index